PRAYERS IN LATER LIFE

Rita F. Snowden – apart from her books – is widely known in many countries. After six years at business, she trained as a deaconess of the New Zealand Methodist Church. She served in turn two pioneer country areas and moved to the largest city for some years of social work during an economic depression. While bedridden with a severe heart condition, she wrote her first book, *Through Open Windows*.

Her extensive travels include five years touring New Zealand, lecturing and introducing books. In Australia she was guest speaker at the Methodist Centenary in Queensland and, some years later, at the Methodist Home Mission Centenary in New South Wales; in a similar working capacity she visited other Australian states including the primitive Inland. She has also travelled widely in Europe, Palestine, the Middle East and Japan.

Miss Snowden has served the world Church – beyond the ministry of her own denomination – with regular broadcasting commitments. She has written and spoken in Britain, Canada and the United States, and in Tonga at the invitation of Queen Salote. She has represented her Church at the World Methodist Conference in Oxford, later being elected the first woman Vice-president of the New Zealand Methodist Church, and President of its Deaconess Association. She is an Hon. Vice-President of the New Zealand Women Writers' Society, a Fellow of The International Institute of Arts and Letters and a member of P.E.N. She was awarded the O.B.E. in the 1976 Honours List. A regular contributor to the *British Weekly* and other periodicals in the English-speaking world, she is the author of more than fifty books for adults and children – three of the most recent being the companion volumes: *A Woman's Book of Prayers*, *Prayers for the Family*, and *Where the Action Is*.

Companion Volumes

Prayers for the Family
A Woman's Book of Prayers
Where the Action Is
RITA F. SNOWDEN

The Plain Man's Book of Prayers
More Prayers for the Plain Man
Prayers for Help and Healing
WILLIAM BARCLAY

PRAYERS
IN LATER LIFE

Rita F. Snowden

COLLINS
FONTANA BOOKS

ACKNOWLEDGEMENTS

The author and publisher wish to acknowledge their indebtedness for permission to use copyright material as follows: 'The Kingdoms of the earth' from *Through the Christian Year* by George F. Bradby; 'Dear Lord, for all in pain' from *Rose from Brier* by Amy Wilson Carmichael © The Dohnavur Fellowship, India. The Bible readings are taken from the Revised Standard Version Bible, copyright 1946, 1952 and © 1971 by the Division of Christian Education, National Council of the Churches of Christ in the USA, and from *The Moffatt Translation of the Bible* published by Hodder & Stoughton Ltd in Great Britain, and in the United States under the title *The Bible: A New Translation* by James Moffatt. Copyright 1954 by James Moffatt. By permission of Harper & Row, Publishers, Inc.

First published in Fontana Books 1974
Third Impression May 1976
© 1974 Rita F. Snowden

Printed in Great Britain
Collins Clear-Type Press
London and Glasgow

Preface

Old age in this Space Age is not easy. If there ever was a time when one thing happened at a time, it's past. Now speed is speedier, noise noisier, peace harder to find.

At the same time, the miracles of medical science are pushing back the frontier of old age – though it has to be met. 'Old age,' says the Book of Wisdom 'is not honoured for length of time, nor measured by number of years.' In our words, it's not something that descends when one reaches a certain age, produces a double chin, or when one becomes eligible for a pension; it's rather something that's woven of all the years. But it is an experience that has special needs – and we are all amateurs here, though many, passing this way, have much to share.

The mounting years come more gently if one has a measure of health; a life-work completed with success and satisfaction; hobbies; a well-stored mind; a curious and cheerful outlook; somewhere nice to live, someone to love. An old Roman Catholic mother superior put this well: 'Lord, thou knowest better than I know myself that I am growing older, and will some day be old. Keep me from getting talkative, and particularly from the fatal habit of thinking I must say something on every subject and on every occasion. Release me from craving to straighten out everybody's affairs. Keep my mind free from the recital of endless details – give me wings to get to the point. I ask for grace enough to listen to the tales of others' pains. Help me to endure them with patience. But seal my lips on my own aches and pains – they are increasing and my love of rehearsing them is becoming sweeter as the years go by. Teach me the glorious lesson that occasionally it is possible that I may be mistaken. Keep me reasonably sweet: I do not want to be a saint – some of them are so hard to live with –

but a sour old woman is one of the crowning works of the devil. Make me thoughtful, but not moody; helpful, but not bossy. With my vast store of wisdom, it seems a pity not to use it all – but thou knowest, Lord, that I want a few friends at the end. Amen.'

This prayer, one sees plainly, despite denomination and sex, is one we can each pray, as are the prayers that follow in this book.

Many of our day's ageing people live in church homes, or community settlements. Some years ago, my old Principal made this change – and wrote me a charming letter. Long retired, she said: 'The church here has a lovely new home, where nursing and loving-kindness are turned on all day long. I've decided that it's a good time to move – I'm just ninety, and old age could set in any time now.' Of course, it could!

Her letters still come – and the arrival of each remains a delight – suspending business in our house for half an hour at least. Lately, she wrote: 'I'm having bother with my eyes, and I'm deaf now. But there are two dear old Methodist ministers here who come and pray with me – they're deaf, too, and can't hear a word that's said. But thank goodness, there is One present, Who understands the lot of us!'

Goethe was past eighty when he finished *Faust*; Cato learned Greek at eighty – like an old friend of mine, 'filling her mind with the best to the last,' to read her New Testament in the original. And any number we know of have kept them company – famous names, many of them – Sir Winston Churchill, Lord Russell, Grandma Moses the artist, not to mention many less distinguished. Good health has helped, of course, and money enough to meet modest needs; but really, it's a matter of spirit.

'The great use of life,' said William James, 'is to spend it for something that outlasts it.'

RFS

FIRST DAY

In the morning

O God, my Father, I am glad to be alive, and here –
I waken much earlier these mornings. I seem not
to need so much sleep, as at one time. Though by
night, I'm glad enough of my bed. My energies
are not what they used to be – but thou dost understand that. Once, I could go on and on – but I
can't now. Others must take their turn. But here I
am, putting myself first – please forgive me.

Hear my thanks for all that I have experienced –
for my place in life, work to do, and dear ones;
for the fertility of the earth, and beauty all
about me;
for the history of great deeds, and good men
and women;
for difficulties met with courage, and overcome;
for laughter and fun, and the prattle of little
children.

Let me make my own small contribution to that
grand total today. For Christ's sake.   AMEN

In the evening

O God, I give thanks at day's end for food and
exercise; for company, and many interests;
I give thanks for talk of old days, and for hope of
the future.
I ask forgiveness for anything amiss today –
if I have been unmindful of blessings;
if I have been short of patience;

8

if I have allowed self-pity to take charge.
By thy mercy, cleanse me of these sins before I
come to my sleep –

if I have caused hurt to any other;

if I have talked too much, and played up my
importance;

if I have shown unreadiness to co-operate.

In thy mercy, forgive me, before I come to my
sleep, and keep me relaxed and trusting through
the night hours. In Christ's power and presence.

AMEN

Daily Reading

In the beginning was the Word, and the Word was
with God, and the Word was God. He was in the
beginning with God; all things were made through
him, and without him was not anything made that
was made. In him was life, and the life was the
light of men. The light shines in the darkness, and
the darkness has not overcome it . . . He came to
his own home, and his own people received him
not. But to all who received him, who believed in
his name, he gave power to become children of
God; who were born, not of blood nor of the will of
the flesh nor of the will of man, but of God.

John 1.1–5,11–13. *Revised Standard Version*

In the morning

O God, creator of all, I thank thee for another day –
   let it find me full of love, and quiet joy;
   let me use well the simple things I have;
   let me take good care of my health as a gift from
      thee.

Let me do my share today to make this a happy
place –
   using my strength for others who have less;
   using my experience to add interest to con-
      versation;
   using my money to serve others whom I cannot
      otherwise reach.

Let the spirit of Christ be seen in my bearing this
day –
   making life richer for all about me;
   making the discouraged to know new hope;
   making our total offering of life, part of thine on-
      going purpose.

Bless today all dear to me, and keep them within
the hollow of thy hand.   AMEN

In the evening

O God, I am tired. Yet this has been a good day –
   forgive me for my bright promises of this morning
      that I have not kept;
   forgive me where I have felt a little superior,
      ready to smile at others' poor efforts;

forgive me for the letter I've put off writing, out of sheer laziness.

Bless those at work in the big world of affairs, where I no longer have a place –

all whose work is becoming more than a match for their strength;

all whose work today has been dull, and without satisfaction;

all whose promise of promotion is long in coming.

So, gather us in, as we come to our sleep. Refresh us, and bring us to a new day, secure in thy love and keeping. AMEN

Daily Reading

The Lord is my shepherd; I shall not want.

He maketh me to lie down in green pastures: he leadeth me beside the still waters.

He restoreth my soul: he leadeth me in the paths of righteousness for his name's sake.

Yea, though I walk through the valley of the shadow of death, I will fear no evil: for thou art with me; thy rod and thy staff they comfort me.

Thou preparest a table before me in the presence of mine enemies: thou anointest my head with oil; my cup runneth over.

Surely goodness and mercy shall follow me all the days of my life: and I will dwell in the house of the Lord for ever.

Psalm 23. *Authorized Version*

THIRD DAY

In the morning

O God, my Father eternal, it is wonderful to know
that thou art in charge of this world –
so many changes have come since I was young –
some of them hard to accept;
so many companions of my years are no longer
here – I seem at times so much alone;
so many frightening events get into the headlines
of the paper that I tremble for the world.
Yet I know that nothing can happen to any of us,
without thy knowledge –
no new experience can take thee by surprise;
no human need be mine, outside thy power to
meet it;
no coming event out-match thy love for me, in
Christ.
Hold today in thy great keeping all dear to me –
especially the over-worked; the worried, the un-
well, any who, still living together, find their hearts
have drifted apart, any without my religious confidence. In Christ's name, I offer this all-embracing
prayer.   AMEN

In the evening

O Father, forgive me, if today I have tackled things
too solemnly – forgetting fun and laughter;
forgive me, if I have been so busy with my own
small affairs, that I failed others about me;

forgive me if I have behaved as one without faith,
  and the experience of years, to back it up;
forgive me if I have grown casual about the deep
  things by which my spirit really lives.
Accept my thanks for the beauty of gardens, trees
and skies; for fragrance, and the lovely shapes of
things in nature; for songs – old-fashioned and
true – for stories and books, and for modern com-
forts – electric-blankets, electric light, and TV.
So may I come to my rest, and blessed, lie down in
peace.   AMEN

Daily Reading

O Lord our Lord, how excellent is thy name in all
  the earth! who hast set thy glory above the
  heavens.
Out of the mouth of babes and sucklings hast thou
  ordained strength because of thine enemies, that
  thou mightest still the enemy and the avenger.
When I consider thy heavens, the work of thy
  fingers, the moon and the stars, which thou hast
  ordained;
What is man, that thou art mindful of him? and
  the son of man, that thou visitest him?
For thou hast made him a little lower than the angels,
  and hast crowned him with glory and honour.

O Lord our Lord, how excellent is thy name in all
the earth!   Psalm 8.1–5,9. *Authorized Version*

FOURTH DAY

In the morning

O God, utterly to be trusted, all who share with me life today, get that gift from thee –

Let this day be a good day, unspoiled by self-centredness;

unspoiled by jealousy;

unspoiled by casualness.

Let this day be a good day, full of thanksgiving;

full of faith and trust;

full of loving consideration.

Let this day be a good day, bringing me some new idea;

bringing me growth in friendship;

bringing me a chance to serve others.

So may thy will be done in my life today, bringing a glow of goodness over all in the name of Christ.

AMEN

In the evening

In health and sickness, in joy and sorrow, thou art always with me –

lovable, dependable, near;

shown in thy full glory in Jesus Christ;

known to me in words and actions of good people.

Help me to sort out the things that really matter in this life –

casting away the unworthy;

strengthening with my will all that is fine;

sharing with others as I am able, thy love and
peace.
Let not my sense of well-being lure me to a dependence on human strength –
bless all who serve the sick;
bless all who counsel the worried;
bless all who serve thee through the needs of
youth and childhood. AMEN

Daily Reading
It is good to give thanks to the Lord,
to sing praises to thy name, O Most High;
to declare thy steadfast love in the morning,
and thy faithfulness by night,
to the music of the lute and the harp,
to the melody of the lyre.
For thou, O Lord, hast made me
glad by thy work;
at the works of thy hands I sing for joy.

How great are thy works, O Lord!
Thy thoughts are very deep!
The dull man cannot know,
The stupid cannot understand this.
Psalm 92.1–6. *Revised Standard Version*

FIFTH DAY

In the morning

O God, I would not take my good sleep for granted –
as I give thanks,

> I remember the sleepless;
> I remember the homeless;
> I remember the distraught.

The returning light, and all nature speak of thy
creative care –

> the trees and flowers;
> the birds and whispering winds;
> the playfulness and trust of pets.

Be especially near to all who face hard tasks today,
a little afraid –

> those going to a new school;
> those meeting strangers;
> those unsure of their capacities.

We are all thy children of this earth family; teach
us how to live, to love, and rejoice. In the name of
Christ.   AMEN

In the evening

From time beyond man's remembering, the night
has gathered in the weary for rest – the wild
creatures flying homeward on tired wings; turning
for known shelter with darkness; glad of provided
sheds and barns where they are.

And men and women and little children have
hushed their hearts at this time;

> to hear thy voice speak more surely;
> to recollect the doings and thoughts of day;

to seek forgiveness and restoration.
And I am thy child, too; needing these same
blessings –

    hear my simple prayer as I bow my head;
    forgive my foolishness, my loveless-ness;
    surround me with thy confidence and peace.
And in sweet, unworried sleep, bring me renewal,
I pray.   AMEN

Daily Reading

Seeing the crowds, he went up on the mountain,
and when he sat down his disciples came to him.
And he opened his mouth and taught them,
saying:

'Blessed are the poor in spirit, for theirs is the
kingdom of heaven. Blessed are those who mourn,
for they shall be comforted. Blessed are the meek,
for they shall inherit the earth. Blessed are those
who hunger and thirst for righteousness, for they
shall be satisfied. Blessed are the merciful, for they
shall obtain mercy. Blessed are the pure in heart,
for they shall see God. Blessed are the peacemakers,
for they shall be called sons of God.

Blessed are those who are persecuted for
righteousness' sake, for theirs is the kingdom of
heaven. Blessed are you when men revile you and
persecute you and utter all kinds of evil against you
falsely on my account. Rejoice and be glad, for your
reward is great in heaven, for so men persecuted
the prophets who were before you.'

      Matthew 5.1–12. *Revised Standard Version*

In the morning
O Lord, I am slow to learn some things – but thou hast given me a new morning, in which to try once more –
>teach me how better to love, today;
>teach me how better to offer friendship;
>teach me how to sustain enthusiasm.

It is useless to pretend that I have always loved others as I might –
>that I have worshipped thee with my whole heart;
>that I have never gossiped, to others' un-doing;
>that I have kept up my courage in times of testing.

But every new day from thee, is a new beginning –
>save me from weakness of will, today;
>save me from stubbornness;
>save me from vanity.

In every situation, let me seek first thy will, and thy glory. For Christ's sake.   AMEN

In the evening
O God, I give thanks just now, for letters that have come through the post –
>for walks, with refreshing exercise;
>for books and magazines and music;
>for laughter, and the oft-told tale.

I give thanks for good meals, attractively spread;
>for comfortable chairs, cushions, and beds;

for memories of by-gone days;
    for the expectation of delights ahead.
I rejoice in my friends in this life – and beyond it;
    for all tied to me by bonds of relationship;
    for neighbours, and acquaintances;
    for shopkeepers and servants ministering to my
        needs.
Grant me thy gift of peace, as sleep comes now, for
Christ's sake.   AMEN

Daily Reading

What shall we then say to these things? If God be
for us, who can be against us? He that spared not
his own Son, but delivered him up for us all, how
shall he not with him also freely give us all things?
. . . Who shall separate us from the love of Christ?
shall tribulation, or distress, or persecution, or
famine, or nakedness, or peril, or sword? As it is
written, For thy sake we are killed all the day long;
we are accounted as sheep for the slaughter. Nay,
in all these things we are more than conquerors
through him that loved us. For I am persuaded, that
neither death, nor life, nor angels, nor principalities,
nor powers, nor things present, nor things to come,
nor height, nor depth, nor any other creature,
shall be able to separate us from the love of God,
which is in Christ Jesus our Lord.

Romans 8.31–2,35–9. *Authorized Version*

In the morning

O God, the morning comes with its sweet renewal for those who sleep well –

I do not forget the sick, and restless; the pilots and firemen and caretakers on duty;

I do not forget the doctors, nurses and hospital staffs.

Bless today especially, all parents of little children;

all teachers and masters in schools and colleges;

all men and women serving on the land;

all at business, caught up within complex dealings.

Bless especially those bearing the burdens of government – newspaper men and women – editors, reporters;

all serving in lands newly come to freedom;

all faced with great choices, for the good of all.

I rejoice that in thy sight, all service is of a piece – there is no sacred or secular – but all is of significance.

For peacemakers I pray, especially this day – in my own small setting, let me join them. In thy name.   AMEN

In the evening

Eternal Father, all the moods, and needs of my life are known to thee – possessed of thy strength, I have come to this hour; sharing thy gifts with others has brought joy; shouldering responsibilities, new dependence.

Let the sacredness of persons about me remain clear; the comfort of others be my concern; the experiences of others my enrichment.

Bless especially, as I think of them, all preachers and missionaries known to me in this land, and afar; all young people in hostels and institutions; all old friends, come to the calm eventide of life.

We are all thy children – faltering often, forsaking the highway for the less challenging. Forgive us, I pray; and grant us strength to try again; with a clear purpose, beating strong within. So teach us how to live well, for Christ's sake.　　AMEN

Daily Reading

O God, thou art my God, I seek thee,
　my soul thirsts for thee;
my flesh faints for thee,
　as in a dry and weary land where no water is.
So I have looked upon thee in the sanctuary,
　beholding thy power and glory.
Because thy steadfast love is better than life,
　my lips will praise thee.
So I will bless thee as long as I live;
　I will lift up my hands and call on thy name.
My soul is feasted as with marrow and fat,
　and my mouth praises thee with joyful lips,
when I think of thee upon my bed,
　and meditate on thee in the watches of the night.
　　　　　Psalm 63.1–6. *Revised Standard Version*

EIGHTH DAY

In the morning

O God, thou hast given me all that I have as I waken – breath in my lungs, strength in my body, thoughts in my mind, and the power to commune with thyself, in prayer –

Thou hast made me a person – endowed with a greater life than the wild creatures of earth know;

a mind that can reach out beyond the present moment;

a spirit fashioned for thine eternal presence;

a will that surrendered to thyself can be handled again in strength.

Bless all beneath this roof, this day; and bring us all to our resting-beds, without shame, or regret. So may thy living kingdom be served, here and now.

AMEN

In the evening

O Lord, scatter every excuse of frailty and foolish choice, as I bow my head in thy presence. I have known better how to love and to forgive and to serve, than I have succeeded in making part of my life.

But thou canst make the weak strong, and the strong gentle; thou canst forgive the prodigal, and provide the fatted calf of welcome, with the best robe, ring and shoes.

In this quiet place, life reminds me that I was born to belong – that my heart can never find its peace save in thy fatherly presence. Let me waste no time in the far country.

I pray also for any whom I know, lost not in foolish choice but in rebellion. Open his heart to share in the merry-making, when the lost son and the Father are re-united.

Hold with thy loving heart all whom I love; and think of at this moment. In thy presence is fulness of joy; and at thy right hand are pleasures for evermore.

Daily Reading

Whither shall I go from thy spirit? or whither shall
   I flee from thy presence?
If I ascend up into heaven, thou art there: if I make
   my bed in hell, behold, thou art there.
If I take the wings of the morning, and dwell in the
   uttermost parts of the sea;
Even there shall thy hand lead me, and thy right
   hand shall hold me.
If I say, Surely the darkness shall cover me; even the
   night shall be light about me.
Yea, the darkness hideth not from thee; but the
   night shineth as the day: the darkness and the
   light are both alike to thee.

Psalm 139.7–12. *Authorized Version*

In the morning

As I open my eyes, O God, my heart rises towards thee, in praise –

> for the peace that here surrounds me;
> for fresh air and light;
> for the beauty and promise of the skies.

I rejoice in all growing, knowing things –

> grasses and gardens;
> trees on roadsides;
> birds on top-most twigs and lines.

Most of all, I rejoice in the power of conscious thought –

> given to men and women since the dawn of time,
> given to little children and youths;
> given to *me*.

Teach us how to live well, as members of the world family –

> that we may add to the beauty about us, inward beauty;
> that we may love and treasure true values;
> that we may serve thee truly.

AMEN

In the evening

O God, the blessings I ask for myself at day's end,

> I ask for others whom I know and love;
> I ask for the lonely and frustrated;
> I ask for the wilful and irresponsible.

Make more real to me my foolishness – and thy
forgiveness –

> show me the secret of life in Jesus Christ;
> show me great men and women, living humbly
> with him;
> show me gifted leaders, serving for very joy.

So let us all live, and go about our business, as sons
and daughters of the Most High – depending on
thee alone.   AMEN

Daily Reading

In a great house there are not only vessels of gold
and silver but also of wood and earthenware, and
some for noble use, some for ignoble. If any one
purifies himself from what is ignoble, then he will be
a vessel for noble use, consecrated and useful to the
master of the house, ready for any good work. So
shun youthful passions and aim at righteousness,
faith, love, and peace, along with those who call
upon the Lord from a pure heart. Have nothing to
do with stupid, senseless controversies; you know
that they breed quarrels. And the Lord's servant
must not be quarrelsome but kindly to every one,
an apt teacher, forbearing, correcting his opponents
with gentleness . . . I charge you in the presence of
God and of Christ Jesus who is to judge the living
and the dead, and by his appearing and his kingdom.

2 Timothy 2.20–5,4.1. *Revised Standard Version*

TENTH DAY

In the morning
Gracious Lord, thou hast fashioned my body, mind and heart to respond to the new day.
I bring with my first words, thanks for the commonplace joys – a comfortable bed, hot water, clothes and food.
In my following of Christ I falter so often, and so easily, that today I ask not for new truths, but for strength to live up to those I know.
If doubts attack my faith, lingering in the shady corners of my mind, grant me the central certainty of thy love, and care.
Lead me out beyond my own limited wisdom, to thy great wisdom; beyond my own limited interests, to thy great on-going purpose.
Bless all under this roof today – that our home may be beautiful within, as without, ministering to life.
If problems appear, resolve them in the love and spirit of Jesus Christ.   AMEN

In the evening
As the day closes, I know more surely than ever before that in thee I live and move and have my being.
Thou hast set me to live in this time and place – and I bring thee thanks for this wonderful experience.
Thou hast not meant me to walk alone, but in the helpful fellowship of others I call 'my friends'.

Grant new understanding to all who find life difficult as the years go by and infirmities multiply.

Deliver us from self-pity that blinds us to the needs of others about us, day by day.

Come, when we are sad, to comfort us; when we are dull, to brighten us; when we are tired, to refresh our spirits.

All my loved ones I commend to thee, knowing full well that they were loved of thee, before ever I loved them.

Gather us in – we are all thy children.   AMEN

Daily Reading

Let not your heart be troubled: ye believe in God, believe also in me. In my Father's house are many mansions: if it were not so, I would have told you. I go to prepare a place for you. And if I go and prepare a place for you, I will come again, and receive you unto myself; that where I am, there ye may be also. And whither I go ye know, and the way ye know. Thomas saith unto him, Lord, we know not whither thou goest; and how can we know the way? Jesus saith unto him, I am the way, the truth, and the life: no man cometh unto the Father, but by me. If ye had known me, ye should have known my Father also: and from henceforth ye know him, and have seen him.

John 14.1–7. *Authorized Version*

ELEVENTH DAY

In the morning

O God Almighty, it is amazing to remember that as the earth turns, the voice of prayer is never silent –

    I use the words that come easiest to me;

    others do the same, in this country;

    and in countless others where I have never been.

We ask earnestly and urgently for a more peaceful world –

    for good home-makers, and parents;

    for wise teachers;

    and preachers and priests dedicated to thine on-going Gospel.

Have mercy on all who cause needless suffering to themselves –

    strengthen the ties that bind good men and women;

    lighten with joy and laughter the gloomy and dull;

    and hold us all within the beauty of thy purpose. AMEN

In the evening

When the light dies, and night comes like a soft garment, give me a renewed sense of thy nearness.

Forgive any foolish things that have crept today into our human relationships.

Let the lovely things seen and heard, linger in our minds as matters for thankfulness.

Sustain those I know who are ill, or troubled, or involved in accidents of any kind.

Bless all who minister to them with gifts of understanding, skill, and love.

Give to us all the precious gift of hope – and if the recovery of health is not to be, go with us through the dark portals to life.

Thou hast placed in our frail hands for a time, the strands whose issues are in eternity. Our trust is in thee alone.   AMEN

Daily Reading

The Lord is gracious and merciful, slow to anger, and abounding in steadfast love.

The Lord is good to all, and his compassion is over all that he has made.

All thy works shall give thanks to thee, O Lord, and all thy saints shall bless thee!

They shall speak of the glory of thy kingdom, and tell of thy power,

to make known to the sons of men thy mighty deeds, and the glorious splendour of thy kingdom.

Thy kingdom is an everlasting kingdom, and thy dominion endures throughout all generations.

The Lord is faithful in all his words, and gracious in all his deeds.

The Lord upholds all who are falling, and raises up all who are bowed down.

Psalm 145.8–14. *Revised Standard Version*

In the morning

O God, give me strength today for what I have to
do –
> things that I have already planned;
> things that may come suddenly upon me;
> things that involve others as well.

Bless any who may come over my doorstep –
> that I may meet them with a smile;
> listen to their talk, with interest and patience;
> lend them my energies in any way I can, to add
> to their own.

So bring us to our resting-beds at the day's end,
unruffled, with gratitude for what the day has
brought;
> kinder in our judgements;
> more generous in our self-giving.

For Christ's sake.   AMEN

In the evening

From ancient times, men and women have sought
thee –
> beside strange altars, in strange tongues;
> in times of festivity, and grief;
> with infants and children, youth, and the
> mature.

And I do the same now – in my own way, that I
understand, in this place that I know so well.
> I bless thee for the changing seasons of the
> year, each with its beauty.

I rejoice in the endless variety of life – for books
and papers, flowers and trees.
Hold me in the hollow of thy hand, as I come to my
rest – and in sleep grant me sweet renewal, for
Christ's sake.   AMEN

Daily Reading
Abide in me, and I in you. As the branch cannot
bear fruit by itself, unless it abides in the vine,
neither can you, unless you abide in me. I am the
vine, you are the branch. He who abides in me, and
I in him, he it is that bears much fruit, for apart
from me you can do nothing. If a man does not
abide in me, he is cast forth as a branch and withers;
and the branches are gathered, thrown into the fire
and burned. If you abide in me, and my words
abide in you, ask whatever you will, and it shall be
done for you. By this my Father is glorified, that you
bear much fruit, and so prove to be my disciples. As
the Father has loved me, so have I loved you;
abide in my love. If you keep my commandments,
you will abide in my love, just as I have kept my
Father's commandments and abide in his love.
These things I have spoken to you, that my joy may
be in you, and that your joy may be full.

John 15.4–11. *Revised Standard Version*

THIRTEENTH DAY

In the morning

O God, I bless thee for this wonderful world –
 for the freshness of each morning;
 for the bright light of midday;
 for the sweet calm of evening.
I bless thee for thy sustaining presence through the years –
 in my high days and holidays;
 in times of testing and puzzlement;
 in times of joy and accomplishment.
So as time goes on, I have confidence – I cannot fall outside thy care –
 in weakness and sickness of body;
 in aloneness when friends pass on;
 in the experience of death, gateway to the larger life.
All the way, I am secure in thy love and keeping;
and I give glory to thy name.   AMEN

In the evening

I bless thee, O God, for thy divine word – a light upon my way –
 for the challenge of the prophets;
 the poems of the psalmists;
 and the history of the past.
Most of all, I bless thee for the revelation through Jesus –
 for his glowing parables;
 his strength and tenderness to all;

his redeeming love on the cross.
Above all, I bless thee for his risen power, and
presence –
    triumphant for evermore;
    available to all in need;
    leading us gently to his everlasting presence at
    the end.   AMEN

Daily Reading
And he came to Nazareth, where he had been
brought up; and he went to the synagogue, as his
custom was, on the sabbath day. And he stood up to
read; and there was given to him the book of the
prophet Isaiah. He opened the book and found the
place where it was written, 'The Spirit of the Lord is
upon me, because he has anointed me to preach good
news to the poor. He has sent me to proclaim release
to the captives and recovering of sight to the blind,
to set at liberty those who are oppressed, to proclaim
the acceptable year of the Lord.'
Luke 4.16–19. Revised Standard Version

In the morning

O God, my Father, as dawn ushers in the new day,
make me ready to receive it –

> if it holds routine tasks, keep me eager in
> spirit;
> if it holds temptation, keep me strong to choose
> well;
> if it holds reunion and talk with old friends, use
> it to the glory of thy name.

I remember just now, those cheated of sleep last
night, by worry, by revelry, by illness;

I remember just now, those far from the home they
love; and the dear ones;

I remember just now, those with uncertainty about
their future plans.

It strengthens my courage to know that nothing in
this wide world is outside thy mighty keeping, that
no need of the humblest of thy children is ever
unnoticed.

Do thou weave these things of time into thine eternal
purpose!

AMEN

In the evening

O Father, I'm tired; this has been an exacting day,
full of many things. As I lie quietly in my bed, let me
go over them with thanksgiving –

> the people I met;
> the things said;
> the kindnesses shared.

Sift out any suggestion of intolerance, and any hint
of gossip.
Strengthen the remembrance of things beautiful and
of good report.
So may this day bring gladness to thine heart. And
gather me in to sleep.   AMEN

Daily Reading
I will bless the Lord at all times;
   his praise shall continually be in my mouth.
My soul makes its boast in the Lord;
   let the afflicted hear and be glad.
O magnify the Lord with me,
   and let us exalt his name together!
I sought the Lord, and he answered me,
   and delivered me from all my fears.

O taste and see that the Lord is good!
   Happy is the man who takes refuge in him!

Depart from evil, and do good;
   seek peace, and pursue it.
The eyes of the Lord are toward the righteous,
   and his ears toward their cry.
      Psalm 34.1–4,8,14–15. *Revised Standard Version*

FIFTEENTH DAY

In the morning
O God, I give thanks for thy mercy that has brought
me through all the ups and downs of my life –
   for the problems solved;
   the sufferings endured;
   the joys multiplied.
In this quietness, I would dedicate myself anew to
thy loving purpose –
   grant thine over-plus to my human efforts;
   give me a new measure of the Spirit of Christ;
   let me witness to others who ignore thee.
Set some laughter upon my lips this day, some
tenderness in my touch –
   so may thy will be done,
   and thy kingdom more surely come,
   for Christ's sake.   AMEN

In the evening
Forgive me, eternal Father, if I have been lacking in
love this day –
   if I have shown intolerance;
   if I have abused discrimination;
   if hasty words have spoiled relationships.
Forgive me, if I have gone upon my way, unmindful
of the needs of others –
   the lonely,
   the dull,
   the distraught.

Hear my humble prayer now, for those who do not
pray for themselves –
  those known to me;
  those known to their neighbours;
  those known only to thee. For Christ's sake.

AMEN

Daily Reading

Thy steadfast love, O Lord, extends to the heavens,
  thy faithfulness to the clouds.
Thy righteousness is like the mountains of God,
  thy judgements are like the great deep;
  man and beast thou savest, O Lord.

How precious is thy steadfast love, O God!
  the children of men take refuge in the shadow of
    thy wings.
They feast on the abundance of thy house,
  and thou givest them drink from the river of thy
    delights.
For with thee is the fountain of life;
  in thy light do we see light.

O continue thy steadfast love to those who know
    thee,
  and thy salvation to the upright of heart!

Psalm 36.5–10. Revised Standard Version

In the morning

O God, I've been thinking of a lot of things since I
came awake —

> I'm glad to live in a land where I can read the
> Bible;
> I'm glad to be able to share the thoughts of
> those who wrote it;
> I'm glad to have it now translated into my own
> language.

Support and encourage all still working to make this
possible everywhere;

Strengthen and enlighten publishers and binders
and distributors;

Enable scholars, teachers, and preachers to interpret
its shining truths,

That ignorance may flee, and true salvation come
to men and women.

Let its stories of high and gallant adventure speak to
youth,

And its sustaining revelation through Jesus Christ
summon the mature,

As we share together the hazards and excitements of
this life.

> This is my prayer — in the name of Christ,
> Saviour and Lord. AMEN

In the evening

As the colours of day sink with the sun, and birds fly
homeward on tired wings, I seek my rest in thee, my
God —

> take what has gone to make up the pattern of
> my day,
> and use it to thine honour and glory –
> forgiving, and dropping away all that was
> loveless and foolish.

I bless thee for all those who have given service today without thought of reward; without, in some instances, so much as a word of encouragement. I bless thee for all who have *begun* to serve the living Christ today; I rejoice in those who have remained steadfast in allegiance for years;

> some are men and women, famous and gifted;
> some are humble people like myself – with love.
> Gather us all in, this night, together bringing
> glory to thine ever-wondrous name.   AMEN

Daily Reading

He will not always chide,
  nor will he keep his anger for ever.
He does not deal with us according to our sins,
  nor requite us according to our iniquities.
For as the heavens are high above the earth,
  so great is his steadfast love toward those who fear
    him;
as far as the east is from the west,
  so far does he remove our transgressions from us.
As a father pities his children,
  so the Lord pities those who fear him.
For he knows our frame;
  he remembers that we are dust.
              Psalm 103.9–14. *Revised Standard Version*

In the morning
O God, I'm glad that in this world there are more
good people than bad –
> more cheerful than morose;
> more generous souls than mean.
Sometimes when I read the newspaper it seems for a
moment that it must be the other way round;
> to the loss of thy kingdom,
> to the discouragement of us all.
Help me to think fairly of what I hear and read, and
so get things in perspective.
> To pass on good news as eagerly as ill news.
> To give my support to the beautiful, the good,
> the true.
These things are important to me – because much
more important to thee.   AMEN

In the evening
Sometimes, O Lord, as I look back, my youth and
young adulthood seem far off. But in reality, I
know they are but a moment in the memory of
nations. So many changes have come, so many
habits and standards now are new. It is difficult at
times to have patience with the makers of today.
At the heart of things, I am glad of thine unchang-
ing character – what Jesus was in time, thou art
eternally. He said so! And he encouraged us
reverently to call thee, 'Father'. This is a wonderful
reality – and it involves the brotherhood and

sisterhood of the rest of mankind, thy children. I am sorry for some foolishnesses today – help me to mend them. And send me to my sleep forgiven – and so at peace. AMEN

Daily Reading

I appeal to you therefore, brethren, by the mercies of God, to present your bodies as a living sacrifice, holy and acceptable to God, which is your spiritual worship. Do not be conformed to this world but be transformed by the renewal of your mind, that you may prove what is the will of God, what is good and acceptable and perfect. For by the grace given to me I bid every one among you not to think of himself more highly than he ought to think, but to think with sober judgement, each according to the measure of faith which God has assigned him. For as in one body we have many members, and all the members do not have the same functions, so we, though many, are one body in Christ, and individually members one of another. Having gifts that differ according to the grace given to us, let us use them.

Romans 12.1–6. *Revised Standard Version*

In the morning

O God, the world shouts at me often – through newspaper-headlines, hoardings, radio and TV.

I want now to hear thy 'still small voice' bringing to my mind and heart things everlasting.

Enrich with loving-kindness and joy all whose lives touch mine this day, as we move quietly about our affairs.

Make me gentle in my approach to those who are shy or lonely, lacking the support of dear ones.

Quicken my erratic memory, that I may hold on to good and beautiful things – forgetting all acts of selfishness, words unkind.

Keep especially all ageing today, who have to move where people jostle each other – in crowds, in queues, trains and buses.

Let us meet all surprising situations with patience, and self-control – and reach the day's end with gratitude. For Christ's sake.   AMEN

In the evening

As darkness is drawn about me, and the stars come out, let my trust in thee deepen.

As the interests of the day are recalled, let none that causes thee pain remain unforgiven.

Support with thy secret gifts of strength and calm all who minister to the aged and sick; and all who speed others through the night, by plane, ship and train; all who go 'down to the sea in ships'.

Give good judgement and considerateness to those who travel by road – that our highways may serve the issues of life, and not death.

Comfort those who find themselves in strange settings this night – far from home, in hospital, among strangers.

And so keep us all – because in this life we cannot keep ourselves, now or ever.   AMEN

Daily Reading

When I sit in darkness,
   the Lord will be a light to me . . .
Who is a God like thee, pardoning iniquity
   and passing over transgression
   for the remnant of his inheritance?
He does not retain his anger for ever
   because he delights in steadfast love.
He will again have compassion upon us,
   he will tread our iniquities under foot.
Thou wilt cast all our sins
   into the depths of the sea.
Thou wilt show faithfulness to Jacob
   and steadfast love to Abraham,
as thou hast sworn to our fathers
   from the days of old.

       Micah 7.8b,18–20. *Revised Standard Version*

In the morning

As I waken this morning, gracious Father, I cannot help but think of those I know who face a critical medical report – and are fearful;

I cannot help but think of those who, finding their strength taxed to the utmost, have to make changes in their way of life;

I cannot help thinking of those who will move into a church or community settlement today – and find things strange at first.

> We have so many special needs – and we bring them to thee.
>
> We are glad of the Gospel story proving that none ever went away from our Lord despairing, unhelped.
>
> We are glad of the rich casket of jewels that we call experience, supporting fresh action.

Teach us how better to live today, more lovingly, more faithfully, more hopefully. AMEN

In the evening

O God, my Father, have mercy on me this night, when I come to speak in this quiet place, the things of my heart –

> I have not always the best words under command;
>
> I have not always the readiness to admit faults I know;

I do not always take time enough to listen to
thy word.
But I have no one else to whom I can go – who
understands the secret aspirations I hold; the desire
for service I hold; the need for companionship.
I bless thee for the experience of prayer; for the
Bible;
I bless thee for the experience of saints and
sinners;
I bless thee for the experience of common
worship.
Quicken thy Church this night with a true passion
for the souls of men. And grant to all ministers and
priests, nuns, deaconesses, and lay-people, thy
lively Spirit.   AMEN

Daily Reading
A brother helped is like a strong city,
  but quarrelling is like the bars of a castle.
From the fruit of his mouth a man is satisfied;
  he is satisfied by the yield of his lips.
Death and life are in the power of the tongue,
  and those who love it will eat its fruits.
He who finds a wife finds a good thing,
  and obtains favour from the Lord.
The poor use entreaties,
  but the rich answer roughly.
There are friends who pretend to be friends,
  but there is a friend who sticks closer than a
  brother.
        Proverbs 18.19–24. *Revised Standard Version*

In the morning

O God, let no temptation take me by surprise today
– for I am weak without thee –

> the temptation to sharp speaking, when an-
> other's back is turned;
>
> the temptation to moodiness and irritability;
>
> the temptation to count myself superior and
> outside the rules.

Save me today, as I go about my small affairs,
meeting with others –

> if I am tempted to lower my standards for
> popularity;
>
> if I am tempted to shirk any share of awkward
> tasks;
>
> if I am tempted to put things off, till it is too
> late to act.

Thou knowest my weaknesses, better than anyone
around here – better than I know them myself. So
dare to pray this prayer, seeking thine aid.   AMEN

In the evening

So many simple things delight me during the day
all gifts from thee – and I come to express my
gratitude at nightfall.

So many good people cross my path in an ordinary
day's doings – unthanked often for the kindnesses
they scatter abroad.

So many letters and phone messages and brief
visits from friends lighten the routine of my day
that I could not live without them.

I bless thy creative goodness for all these – and the things of nature – grass and garden and ten thousand surprising living creatures.

The hills and mountains praise thee – let me praise thee too; the rivers and seas rejoice in the life thou hast given them – let me do that too; the prattle of tiny children, and the songs and laughter of young people make thy creation more meaningful – let me add my contribution day by day. For Christ's sake.

AMEN

Daily Reading

So he told them this parable: 'What man of you, having a hundred sheep, if he has lost one of them, does not leave the ninety-nine in the wilderness, and go after the one which is lost, until he finds it? And when he has found it, he lays it on his shoulders, rejoicing. And when he comes home, he calls together his friends and his neighbours, saying to them, "Rejoice with me, for I have found my sheep which was lost." . . .

'Or what woman, having ten silver coins, if she loses one coin, does not light a lamp and sweep the house and seek diligently until she finds it? And when she has found it, she calls together her friends and neighbours, saying, "Rejoice with me, for I have found the coin which I had lost." Just so, I tell you, there is joy before the angels of God over one sinner who repents.'

Luke 15.3–6,8–10. *Revised Standard Version*

In the morning

O God, thou art ever bringing light out of darkness,
strength out of weariness, new beginnings out of
spent energies.

By bedtime last night, I couldn't have done another
thing – and now I am ready once more for what the
day will bring.

> I bless thee for the miracle of returning day;
> I bless thee for colour returned to sky and
> garden;
> I bless thee for breakfast spread out of thy
> world-harvest.

Grant a special sense of thy nearness today to all in
charge of little children; all who tend the sick and
distraught; all who make pretty clothes and wear
them; all who cook attractive meals with a great
deal of care. From the rising of the sun, till the
going down of the same – and on into the night –
keep us within thy mighty care. For Christ's sake.

AMEN

In the evening

I want to give time to thinking of our Lord's
earthly life –

> his modest home in Nazareth;
> Mary busy at her baking;
> the carpenter at his bench.

I give thanks for his keen observation –

> noting the sparrows in the market;

the sheep lost on the mountainside;
the hen and her chickens at the threat of storm.
I give thanks for his attitude to people –
the young couple at their marriage;
Zacchaeus up the tree, nicely hidden;
the fishermen busy on the lake-shore.
But most of all for himself – for his sacrifice – and his rising again.
I marvel that I have not to do with a dead Christ.
I long to love him more deeply;
to serve him more faithfully.   AMEN

Daily Reading

Let this mind be in you, which was also in Christ Jesus: Who, being in the form of God, thought it not robbery to be equal with God: But made himself of no reputation, and took upon him the form of a servant, and was made in the likeness of men: And being found in fashion as a man, he humbled himself, and became obedient unto death, even the death of the cross. Wherefore God also hath highly exalted him, and given him a name which is above every name. That at the name of Jesus every knee should bow, of things in heaven, and things in earth, and things under the earth; And that every tongue should confess that Jesus Christ is Lord, to the glory of God the Father . . . For it is God which worketh in you both to will and to do of his good pleasure. Do all things without murmurings and disputings.

Philippians 2.5–11,13–14. *Authorized Version*

In the morning

The dustman and the doctor and scores of other
helpers are already at work – give them thy blessing
today –

> and to all home-makers;
> and matrons of hospitals and homes;
> strengthen those doing hard work.

Let no remembrance of the faults of yesterday, hold
any of us back from willing service today.

Bless especially those who face the day without the
support of home and loved ones.

Bless all whose lives are dull – with no music or
song in them.

And bless those who can do no work – those who lie
in pain; those who prepare for operations.

Bless and keep us all, in our goings-out, and our
comings-in.   AMEN

In the evening

O God, hear my prayer, as the day draws in, and
darkness comes.

Forgive me that many a bush has flamed with thy
glory today, and I have not shown thee due
reverence.

Forgive me that many an opportunity for friendliness
has found me unready if not unwilling.

Forgive me any self-absorption that has rendered me
unmindful of the needs of those about me.

Forgiven and restored, let me now lie down in peace

Hold in thy keeping all who care for me, all who
  love me.
And bring us eagerly to the new day.   AMEN

Daily Reading
I will extol thee, my God and King,
  and bless thy name for ever and ever.
Every day I will bless thee,
  and praise thy name for ever and ever.
Great is the Lord, and greatly to be praised,
  and his greatness is unsearchable.
One generation shall laud thy works to another,
  and shall declare thy mighty acts.
On the glorious splendour of thy majesty,
  and on thy wondrous works, I will meditate.
Men shall proclaim the might of thy terrible acts,
  and I will declare thy greatness.
They shall pour forth the fame of thy abundant
    goodness,
  and shall sing aloud of thy righteousness.
                Psalm 145.1–7. *Revised Standard Version*

In the morning
O God, I give thee thanks for what I know of thee in the framework of the world –

> through friendly human eyes;
> through books and pictures;
> through music and song.

Bless today all who serve their fellows through acts of neighbourliness –

> through the sharing of gardens;
> through the giving of money;
> through the making of meals.

Bless all today who feel too old and frail to take any active part –

> may their prayers sustain others;
> may their smiles reward others;
> may their long, good lives inspire others.

For Christ's sake, I beseech thee answer this prayer.

AMEN

In the evening
Beyond the darkness that veils my sight, I know there is light –

> beyond pain and suffering, wholeness of life;
> beyond ignorance, in thee, perfect knowledge;
> beyond human frailties and foibles, goodness.

Lift up mine eyes, that here by faith, I may see the king in his beauty – in the world of nature;

> in the life of good people and true;

in the supreme life, death, and rising again of
    Christ. AMEN

Daily Reading

Thus I may speak with the tongues of men and of
angels, but if I have no love, I am a noisy gong or a
clanging cymbal; I may prophesy, fathom all
mysteries and secret lore, I may have such absolute
faith that I can move hills from their place, but if I
have no love, I count for nothing; I may distribute
all I possess in charity, I may give up my body to be
burnt, but if I have no love, I make nothing of it.
Love is very patient, very kind. Love knows no
jealousy; love makes no parade, gives itself no airs,
is never rude, never selfish, never irritated, never
resentful; love is never glad when others go wrong,
love is gladdened by goodness, always slow to expose,
always eager to believe the best, always hopeful,
always patient.

1 Corinthians 13.1–7. *Moffatt Translation*

TWENTY-FOURTH DAY

In the morning

O God, I am glad that I can speak my thought
freely to thee, in prayer
>the things that give me pleasure;
>the things that puzzle and perplex;
>the things that concern me in the present, and
>in the future.

O God I am glad that I am set to live in such a
beautiful world –
>that the darkness and light alike praise thee;
>that energies enough are granted for each day
>that others are here to journey with me in love

Garrison my heart today against fears and failings
common to life –
>strengthen my faith;
>strengthen my love;
>strengthen my witness to thy glory and good-
>ness.
>>AMEN

In the evening

The days seem longer than they used to, O God –
but I am fortunate that I can use some of them for
rest;

It is harder to carry loads, and to walk uphill – but
there are many about me to lend a hand;

My eyes are less able to cope with small type –
but many books are made for those of us growing
old;

My ears do not as readily pick up what is said – but

people are patient, and ready to say things over again.

I bring thee my thanks at this day's end, and I ask thy blessing on all who call me 'friend'. Save us all from being religious at church, and moody and difficult to live with at home. In Christ's name.

AMEN

Daily Reading

Love never disappears. As for prophesying, it will be superseded; as for 'tongues', they will cease; as for knowledge, it will be superseded. For we only know bit by bit, and we only prophesy bit by bit; but when the perfect comes, the imperfect will be superseded. When I was a child, I talked like a child, I thought like a child, I argued like a child; now that I am a man, I am done with childish ways.

At present we only see the baffling reflections in a mirror, but then it will be face to face; at present I am learning bit by bit, but then I shall understand, as all along I have myself been understood. Thus 'faith and hope and love last on, these three,' but the greatest of all is love.

1 Corinthians 13.8–13. Moffatt Translation

In the morning

O God, no two mornings are ever alike – but thou art the same evermore –

> faithful in the keeping of all thy promises;
> fair in all thy judgements;
> full of love and wise concern.

I bless thee for all preachers, teachers and friends through whom I have

> come to know thee through the years;
> come to walk the Christian way;
> come to worship, and to pray, and serve.

Banish from my heart today any lurking grudge and unkind criticism –

> let me live as simply as I pray;
> let me forgive, even as I am forgiven;
> let me witness to thy goodness, sincerely and joyously today. In Christ's strength. AMEN

In the evening

Looking back over today, O Lord, I am led to offer thee praise –

> for the promise of the morning;
> for the kindness of friends;
> for the truth of the Gospel ever sure.

No tongue can bring to thee worthy praise –

> let my life out-match my words;
> let my heart be always towards thee;
> let my Christian witness be consistent.

So bless my coming-in this evening, as thou didst
bless my going-out –
    and in thy mercy remember ——————
    and—————— and ————————————

AMEN

Daily Reading

Then those who feared the Lord spoke with one
another; the Lord heeded and heard them, and a
book of remembrance was written before him of
those who feared the Lord and thought on his
name. 'They shall be mine,' says the Lord of hosts,
my special possession on the day when I act, and I
will spare them as a man spares his son who serves
him. Then once more you shall distinguish between
the righteous and the wicked, between one who
serves God and one who does not serve him.

Malachi 3.16–18. *Revised Standard Version*

In the morning

I praise thee for the return of morning light – for freshness and hope –

> may the hours stretching before me be well used;
>
> may the associations with others be pleasant;
>
> may I come to my rest unashamed and full of joy.

I praise thee for fulfilling in time the promise of redemption –

> for faithful hearts in Palestine who received the Babe;
>
> for the modest carpenter's home in Nazareth;
>
> for men and women responsive to the call of Christ.

I praise thee that many of these are now known to me, through the Gospels –

> ordinary people like myself in many cases;
>
> faulty people, forgiven like myself, and made anew;
>
> forward-looking people, set on the ultimate triumph of thy kingdom. Receive my praise, in Christ's blessed name.   AMEN

In the evening

O God, I am glad that thou hast given evenings – as well as mornings –

> for my body grows tired by this time;
>
> my mind becomes less retentive;

my aches multiply.
So I come to my resting-bed with gratitude, looking
back over the day –

    thankful for friends;

    thankful for flowers and good food;

    thankful for clothes that add warmth and
       dignity.

Let not the happiness of my situation hinder my
spirit of dependence –

    keep me ever mindful of thy goodness;

    ever ready to serve the needs of others;

    ever dependent on thy holy love.   AMEN

Daily Reading

Six days before the Passover, Jesus came to Bethany,
where Lazarus was, whom Jesus had raised from the
dead. There they made him a supper; Martha
served, and Lazarus was one of those at table with
him. Mary took a pound of costly ointment of pure
nard and anointed the feet of Jesus and wiped his
feet with her hair; and the house was filled with the
fragrance of the ointment. But Judas Iscariot, one
of his disciples (he who was to betray him) said,
'Why was this ointment not sold for three hundred
denarii and given to the poor?' This he said, not that
he cared for the poor but because he was a thief, and
as he had the money box he used to take what was
put into it. Jesus said, 'Let her alone, let her keep it
for the day of my burial.'

         John 12.1–7. *Revised Standard Version*

In the morning

Never morning fades to evening, O God, but some heart doth ache —

> but thou art ever at hand to heal and bless;
> thou art ever able to minister through friends;
> thou art ever able to comfort through remembered promises of Scripture.

Save me today from accepting as commonplace, the service of those near me —

> let me be as ready to give as to receive;
> let me express in action the things I know by heart;
> let no one find me unresponsive, uncaring.

Ever-present Lord of life, no need nor distance known to us can separate us from thee.   AMEN

In the evening

As I look back over this day, O God, I know that thou art the source of all good and lovely things that stir my heart —

> thou hast given me a roof over my head;
> thou hast given me food and clothing;
> thou has given me strength to move about.

I like having my pretty personal bits and pieces about me —

> things given me by loved ones;
> things I have bought;
> things I have made.

Let the door of my home – and of my heart – be open
wide enough –
>   to receive those who come,
>   to shut out all light talk and gossip;
>   to give a welcome to the lonely.
In the name of Christ who had no roof of his own
over his earthly head.   AMEN

Daily Reading

For I was an hungred, and ye gave me meat: I was
thirsty, and ye gave me drink: I was a stranger, and
ye took me in: Naked, and ye clothed me: I was sick,
and ye visited me: I was in prison, and ye came unto
me. Then shall the righteous answer him, saying,
Lord, when saw we thee an hungred, and fed thee?
or thirsty, and gave thee drink? When saw we thee
a stranger, and took thee in? or naked, and clothed
thee? Or when saw we thee sick, or in prison, and
came unto thee? And the King shall answer and say
unto them, Verily I say unto you, Inasmuch as ye
have done it unto one of the least of these my
brethren, ye have done it unto me.

>   Matthew 25.35–40. *Authorized Version*

In the morning

I bless thee, O Father, for all the seemingly ordinary things –
>   a cup of tea at rising;
>   a letter through the post;
>   a bunch of flowers for my vase.

I would not take for granted any gift which brings me joy –
>   health and strength and good food;
>   a walk with another in the sunshine;
>   a favourite book passed on by a friend.

With Paul and people of every generation, I join in saying that there is nothing that can separate us –
>   neither height nor depth;
>   neither life nor death.

Thou art worthy of more love than I can bring– accept what I do bring.   AMEN

In the evening

God, my Father, forgive me if today I have acted poorly –
>   making of my virtue a vain glory;
>   thrusting out a small fault, forgetting a greater;
>   removing the mote from my neighbour's eye, forgetting the beam in my own.

I need thy forgiveness continually, or I cannot press forward –

I need thy strength continually, or I cannot face temptation –

I need thy generous spirit within, or I cannot move among my fellows bearing the name of Christian.

Bless, as I remember them now —— and ——
dear to me;

Bless those in special need —— and —— I pray;

Bless especially those thy children who do not acknowledge thee. In the name of Jesus Christ.

AMEN

Daily Reading

Purge me with hyssop, and I shall be clean;
    wash me, and I shall be whiter than snow.

Fill me with joy and gladness;
    let the bones which thou hast broken rejoice.

Hide thy face from my sins,
    and blot out all my iniquities.

Create in me a clean heart, O God,
    and put a new and right spirit within me.

Cast me not away from thy presence,
    and take not thy holy Spirit from me.

Restore to me the joy of thy salvation,
    and uphold me with a willing spirit.

Psalm 51.7–12. Revised Standard Version

In the morning

O God, there is no good and lovely thing but comes
from thee –
>   accept my morning thanks;
>   accept for thy service my renewed energies;
>   accept the unspoken wonder of my heart.

Let me be humble in the use of my powers this day –
>   all my native gifts;
>   all my trained and developed skills;
>   all my spiritual sensibilities.

So may others find in my life today, some reminder
of thy holy love –
>   matching the trust of little children;
>   matching the eagerness of youth;
>   matching the special needs of the mature and
>   the aged.

In the name of Christ who gathered all about him,
I make this prayer.   AMEN

In the evening

O God, there are things that worry me sometimes
at day's end –
>   you know what they are, nobody else does;
>   Show me their true nature ——————————
>   Show me what can be done about them ————

I worry about my health sometimes; help me to be
sensible about it –
>   let me not expend my energies recklessly;
>   let me not fuss over slight symptoms;

let me take advantage of good sun and air.
And give me gentle understanding of those about
who are now frail. Bless with offered skills those
unfit to care for themselves; Especially bless those
newly in hospital, suffering accident and shock.

In the name of the good physician.   AMEN

Daily Reading

But the mercy of the Lord is from everlasting to
   everlasting upon them that fear him, and his
   righteousness unto children's children;

To such as keep his covenant, and to those that
   remember his commandments to do them.

The Lord hath prepared his throne in the heavens;
   and his kingdom ruleth over all.

Bless the Lord, ye his angels, that excel in strength,
   that do his commandments, hearkening unto the
   voice of his word.

Bless ye the Lord, all ye his hosts; ye ministers of his,
   that do his pleasure.

Bless the Lord, all his works in all places of his
   dominion: bless the Lord, O my soul.

               Psalm 103.17–22. *Authorized Version*

In the morning
O God, I will likely meet today some people I have
never met before –
>   let me be out-reaching with a smile;
>   let me show respect for opinions not my own;
>   let me show interest in others' experiences.

O God, let me not pass today, without encouragement, any having a hard time –
>   in my home;
>   in the street as I walk there;
>   in the congregation with whom I worship.

O God, take the words of my lips, and the kindness
in my looks and bearing –
>   and use them to thy glory;
>   strengthening the faint-hearted;
>   supporting the disappointed.

In the name of Christ, the great encourager.   AMEN

In the evening
In this quiet place and time, O God, I would shed
all haste –
>   I would confess my pride;
>   my blundering ways at times;
>   my self-absorption.

Forgive me these faults, as the night brings remembrance –
>   and quicken my better nature;
>   showing helpfulness;
>   and loving-kindness without thought of gain.

Bless especially this night all who lack the common
decencies –
    all alone, and insecure;
    all frail, without proper help;
    all facing death, a little afraid.
Hold us all in your mighty keeping, I ask this night,
O Lord.   AMEN

Daily Reading
'You are the salt of the earth; but if the salt has lost
its taste, how shall its saltness be restored? It is no
longer good for anything except to be thrown out
and trodden under foot by men. You are the light
of the world. A city set on a hill cannot be hid. Nor
do men light a lamp and put it under a bushel, but
on a stand, and it gives light to all in the house.
Let your light so shine before men, that they may
see your good works and give glory to your Father
who is in heaven. Think not that I have come to
abolish the law and the prophets; I have come not
to abolish them but to fulfil them. For truly, I say to
you, till heaven and earth pass away, not an iota,
not a dot, will pass from the law until all is accom-
plished.'

    Matthew 5.13–18. *Revised Standard Version*

In the morning

Heavenly Father, I value this privilege of prayer –
    bringing me, by faith, into thy holy presence –
    lifting up my eyes above earthly things;
    assessing anew my life against thy standards.
Strengthen me against temptation today –
    to take the easy way;
    to choose the showy and the shoddy;
    to be satisfied with half-knowledge.
Support all those I love, throughout this day –
    those still at school;
    those at work;
    those spending the day at home.
In all our comings and goings, keep us alert, ever set on the highest and loveliest in life. For Christ's sake.   AMEN

In the evening

O God, it is wonderful to know that the creator who holds galaxies in space is my Father –
    expressing thy very nature in Jesus Christ;
    speaking through the prophets, men of courage;
    coming near in the sweet intimacies and re-
        sponsibilities of home and family life.
Deliver me from the servitude of things – give me a lasting scale of values –
    that the things which nourish my spirit;
    the things which inform my mind;

the things which strengthen the beautiful and
    good may be my daily choice.
So let me praise thy name in reverence and service,
O Lord! AMEN

Daily Reading
O come, let us sing unto the Lord:
    let us make a joyful noise to the rock of our salva-
       tion.
Let us come before his presence with thanksgiving,
    and make a joyful noise unto him with psalms.
For the Lord is a great God,
    and a great King above all gods.
In his hand are the deep places of the earth:
    the strength of the hills is his also.
The sea is his, and he made it:
    and his hands formed the dry land.
O come, let us worship and bow down:
    let us kneel before the Lord our maker.

Psalm 95.1–6. Authorized Version

I am wakeful, weighed down. Why?
Hast thou not known? hast thou not heard, that the everlasting God, the Lord, the Creator of the ends of the earth, fainteth not, neither is weary.

Isaiah 40.28

'Speak to Him for He hears, and Spirit with spirit can meet –
Closer is He than breathing, and nearer than hands and feet.'   Tennyson

The earth is full of the goodness of the Lord.

Psalm 33.5

O Lord, the day is thine, and the night is thine!

Bishop Andrewes

Let nothing disturb thee;
Let nothing dismay thee;
All things pass:
God never changes.

St Teresa's bookmark

Who shall separate us from the love of Christ? shall tribulation, or distress, or persecution, or famine, or nakedness, or peril, or sword? As it is written, For thy sake we are killed all the day long; we are accounted as sheep for the slaughter. Nay, in all these things we are more than conquerors through him that loved us. For I am persuaded, that neither death, nor life, nor angels, nor principalities, nor powers, nor things present, nor things to come, nor height, nor depth, nor any other creature, shall be able to separate us from the love of God, which is in Christ Jesus our Lord.

Romans 8.35–39

Peace of mind rests on being certain of some basic things. RFS

Christ is a person to be trusted.

Dr Ronald Selby Wright

Prayer does not always banish my difficulty – but it brings it to the place where I am sharing it with Christ. RFS

I am sick and in pain
It does not matter that I cannot hold on to God – he holds on to me. RFS

Even the night shall be light about me. Yea, the darkness hideth not from thee.   Psalm 139.11b–12a

Lord, behold, he whom thou lovest is sick. John 11.3

Our solace in suffering is that the Man of Sorrows is sure to pass this way. Helen Keller

The Kingdoms of the earth go by
    In purple and in gold:
They rise, they flourish, and they die,
    And all their tale is told.
One Kingdom only is divine,
    One banner triumphs still:
Its King, a servant, and its throne
    A Cross upon a Hill.

George F. Bradby

Life's last word is not a cross . . . What is man's slander if God affirms? What is Calvary, if just beyond it lies an Easter morning?

Dr Stanley Jones

Christ the Lord is risen today.   Charles Wesley

I am awaiting a doctor's verdict
But I am not alone. Jesus said: 'Lo, I am with you alway, even unto the end of the world.' (Matthew 28.20.) This looks like 'the end of the world', but I tell myself it isn't.   RFS

Lord, I pray for others – as for myself:
    Dear Lord, for all in pain
      I pray to thee;
    O come and smite again
      Thine enemy.

Give to thy servants skill
  To soothe and bless,
And to the tired and ill
  Give quietness.

And, Lord, to those who know
  Pain may not cease,
Come near, that even so
  They may have peace.
                              Amy Wilson Carmichael

I am afraid, lest I might be afraid
Lord, thou seest what I am, thou seest what I need.
Share with me thy power.   Alistair MacLean

When I fear my faith will fail
  He will hold me fast.
                                      Old Hymn

There were they in great fear, where no fear was.
                                      Psalm 53.5

Faith went to answer the door for Fear – and there
was no one there.   Unknown

The New Testament is full of people like me, knowing what I feel. But full of much more –
Luke 1.13 Fear not, Zacharias.
     1.30 Fear not, Mary.
     2.10 (to the shepherds) Fear not.

5.10 (to Simon) Fear not.
8.50 (to Jairus) Fear not.
12.32 Fear not, little flock.

My loved-one has died
Year by year we are being led towards a life that is too big for this world to contain.

Rev. Dorothy Wilson

Jesus said: 'I am come that they might have life, and that they might have it more abundantly.'

John 10.10

What shall separate us from the love of Christ? shall . . . life, *shall death? Nay*!   St Paul

I know not what the future hath
Of marvel or surprise,
Assured alone that life and death
His mercy underlies.

I know not where his islands lift
Their fronded palms in air,
I only know I cannot drift
Beyond his love and care.

Whittier

Jesus said: 'I am the resurrection, and the life: he that believeth in me, though he were dead, yet shall he live.'   John 11.25

Then Jesus gave a loud cry and said, 'Father, into thy hands I commit my spirit'; and with these words he died.   Luke 23.46 *New English Bible*

How should I fear to die?
Have I not seen
The colour of a small butterfly,
The silver sheen
Of breaking waves and a wood-dove's wings?

Have I not marked the coat
Of mouse and deer,
The shape of flowers, the thrush's specked throat –
And shall I fear
To fall into the hands that made these things?

Teresa Hooley

Jesus said: 'Because I live, ye shall live also.' (John 14.19) It is not much to say – but knowing him, it is all we need.   RFS

Think of –
Stepping on shore, and finding it Heaven!
Of taking hold of a hand, and finding it God's hand,
Of breathing new air, and finding it celestial air,
Of feeling invigorated, and finding it immortality,
Of passing from storm and tempest to an unbroken
    calm,
Of waking up, and finding it Home.

Unknown

I will give thanks as I lie awake
This is the day which the Lord hath made; we will rejoice and be glad in it. Psalm 118.24

Martin Rinkart raised his voice in thanksgiving, in a time of pestilence and famine:

> Now thank we all our God,
>   With heart and hands and voices,
> Who wondrous things hath done,
>   In whom his world rejoices;
> Who from our mother's arms,
>   Hath blessed us on our way,
> With countless gifts of love,
>   And still is ours today.

Looking back, G. K. Chesterton recalled a time of muddlement and confusion when he 'hung on to the remains of religion by one thin thread of thanks'. I can do that now.

And whatever life faces me with, I can be sure that 'The eternal God is my refuge, and underneath are the everlasting arms.' Deuteronomy 33.27

Prayers for Special Days

For Christmas

O God, my heart is full of joy this morning at the thought of all children everywhere, excitedly giving and receiving gifts.

I think too of all the parents I know who are as busy preparing meals and welcoming friends.

I bless thee for all who have so far remembered me with cards and messages and gifts. Let me not overlook the friendless and hungry.

I give thanks for those who have spared time to move around singing carols.

I give thanks for the brightness and beauty of the decorations everywhere.

But most of all, I rejoice in him whose birthday it is, Christ my Lord!

Bless everyone gathered in church today, the world round, to sing his praises!   AMEN

For New Year's Day

Lord of life, I bring my thanks to thee, at the day's beginning – the year's beginning.

Looking back, there have been so many things for which to give thanks –

    the companionship of those I love;

    the talk and company of friends near and far;

    experiences full of interest and surprise.

    I remember flowers and trees and things of nature –

    I remember the trust of little children;

I remember the confidence and thanks of
    people in need.
I give thanks for the gift of health and home;
I give thanks for faith that has overcome fears;
I look forward to this New Year's gifts with
    eager hope.
In the name and power of Christ Jesus.   AMEN

For Easter Day

Almighty God, my heart is full of joy today, triumph-
ing over the uncertainty and sorrow and hate of
Good Friday –
I give thanks for the little company of the faithful
who found their way to the tomb in the garden on
the first Easter morning –
    for their meeting with the risen Lord;
    for his recognition of those seeking him;
    for the certainty of life more real than death.
Give this same assurance to all of us today who
gather for worship the world round, in old lands and
new –
    let the joy of music and hymns echo in our lives;
    let darkness and superstition and misery flee;
    let the power and love of Christ overcome our
        sin.   AMEN

Whitsunday

O God, let the lasting Spirit of Jesus live in me today –
    quickening my love of thee;
    stirring my love for others about me;

giving me concern for those afar, in need.
Again and again I long for strength to live more
joyously –
    to replace dullness with winsomeness;
    to replace fearfulness with faith;
    to replace self-absorption with self-forgetfulness.
Banish by thy Spirit all that denies thy supreme love
and purpose –
    all superiority;
    all shabby dealings;
    all disloyalty.
So may new life come to thy Church and peace and
joy to thy world.   AMEN

All Saints' Day

O God, I look back over a long life, to remember
many whom I have met –
    I give thanks especially for saints without
        haloes;
    for thy message on their lips and in their lives;
    for their steadfastness and self-forgetfulness.
I remember too those of whom I have read or been
told –
    belonging to distant places where I have never
        been;
    living in early times when history's edges were
        blurred;
    under the domination of ignorant and cruel
        leaders.
I marvel that in thy mercy, I am called now to a
place in the sainthood of all believers –

in this place where each day finds me;

within the limitations of my own personality;

dependent, as saints have always been, on thy
supreme strength.

Enable me to contribute my share this day I pray,
towards thy great on-going purpose. In Christ's
name.   AMEN

My Birthday

O God, my Father, I can hardly believe that the
months have slipped by so quickly.

I give thanks for thy supporting love all through
them to this hour.

Some things I have said might have been better un-
said – forgive me.

Some things I have done might have been better un-
done – forgive me.

I give thee praise for family, and friends;

I give thee praise for interests and leisure;

I give thee praise for interesting talks, and for the
ministry of silence.

Go with me, I pray thee, into the unknown ways of
this new year –

give me strength of body enough for each day;

give me grace of spirit to behave well;

give me courage and strength when things are
hard.

So keep me in all my goings-out and my comings-in,
now and always.   AMEN